www.karlssen.com

BUILDING A
MOTIVATED
SALES TEAM

KARLSSEN

THE ENERGY EFFICIENT WAY
TO FIRE UP YOUR PEOPLE

Berne Group

Contents

CONDITIONS AND INCENTIVES 9

Aunt Emerald and Aunt Gretchen.......................... 11
Motivation in sales... 13
Incentives and conditions 14
Your motivational levers..................................... 15

Material reward 17

Short term 18
Simple... 19
Certain.. 19
Achievable... 20
Your sales team's targets should be achievable, even if
yours aren't... 21
Go easy on the basic salary............................... 22
Dare you break the curse of the time-bound reward
scheme? 23
Filling the incentive vacuum 24
A guaranteed reward is no incentive................... 26
Don't let the incentive vacuum suck the oxygen from peak
performance 26

Job satisfaction.. 29

Allocate work intelligently 29
Make the workplace a bit more like prison 31
Make it a bit more like Mars.............................. 31
Team spirit 33

Mix things up..35

Status 37

Recognition and praise 38
Ownership..39
Career advancement...41
Promotions don't need to include line management........42

Security 43

THE MOTIVATING SALES MANAGER 45

Getting it done..47
Focus most on your "middle 70%" 47
Pull each of the levers and people will self-select what motivates them..49

Your behaviour...51

Have a plan..52
Beat inertia..53
Make sure they understand you're serious.......53
Remember people care more about themselves than they do about you..54
Give feedback effectively..................................54
Win a lot...56
Don't be a stool pigeon.....................................57
If team leadership needs to take second place, delegate it 58
If you can't delegate, get your ducks in a row....59

Self motivation...61

Physician heal thyself..61
Get your mojo back...61
Fail your way to victory..64
Work through the dip 66
Quit often and early...69
Your big potatoes and your peanuts.................................70
Complete your high leverage activities first 71
Positive thinking and the river of excrement...................73
Help others become self motivated.................................76
The winning attitude..76

Checklist: Conditions and incentives 79
Checklist: The motivating sales manager..........................81
About Karlssen 83
www.karlssen.com...83
Index...87

CONDITIONS AND INCENTIVES

Aunt Emerald and Aunt Gretchen

When we were growing up we were lucky enough to live less than a mile away from our two maternal great aunties, Aunt Emerald and Aunt Gretchen. Each lived in semi-detached Edwardian houses at opposite ends of the town, and the two would meet on Wednesdays for a gossip and a toasted teacake, and on Sundays for the eight o'clock mass.

Aunt Emerald was rather elegant, with high cheekbones and beautiful clothes. She was witty and sharply intelligent, and told hilarious, indiscreet stories. Aunt Gretchen was rotund and ever so slightly bearded, with a mischievous twinkle in her eye. She would laugh till the tears rolled down her cheeks.

Both were kind and good, and we loved them dearly and equally. They, in turn, were besotted with us and would light up whenever they saw us, fussing and laughing and bringing out cakes. But as the years went by, something happened.

Aunt Gretchen had an attic room which she had kitted out with a pink beanbag and a dolls house. When our younger sister, Esme, started drawing, Aunt Gretchen furnished the room with crayons and notepads and bits of scrap paper, and when she entered her teens a battered old CD player appeared, which Esme fed with a steady supply of discs.

Aunt Gretchen kept a jar of biscuits which was always full, and her fridge seemed to boast a limitless supply of pop. When her nephews slept overnight at Aunt Gretchen's house, they were allowed to stay up half an hour past their bedtime and take Horlics up to bed with them.

Naturally our dad doted on his wife, our mother, but she wasn't terribly keen on football. At Aunt Gretchen's there was a flat screen TV and an open invitation to make full use of it.

As the years went by we saw less of our great aunts, but we seemed to make time to pop round to Aunt Gretchen's. For the boys this became more frequent when she cleared out her garage and installed a pool table. For Esme the attic room continued to be a sanctuary right through her teens, especially since Gretchen had a liberal attitude towards boyfriends. And during the World Cup and European Championships we probably saw more of Dad at Aunt Gretchen's than we did at home.

Aunt Emerald continued to receive the obligatory visits, during which everyone remembered how much they liked her. She dropped hints that perhaps they could see her more often, and after a while the hints turned to requests and the requests turned to rebukes.

But Aunt Gretchen didn't need to beg, bully, persuade or charm us into visiting. She created a set of conditions and offered a series of incentives that guaranteed we would visit as often as we could. She also understood that we are all motivated by different things. A visit to Aunt Gretchen's house appealed to different people for different reasons. And because she was so good at understanding what *we* wanted,

Aunt Gretchen got what *she* wanted. She would have been a great Sales Director.

Motivation in sales

If you've worked in sales for more than five minutes you won't need convincing about the link between motivation and success. A motivated sales team can overcome all sorts of obstacles (including poor strategy, weak product, awful market, strong competition). An unmotivated team can squander even the best opportunities.

The closest analogy to the sales manager is probably the professional sports coach. Your personal success depends upon the performance of a group of talented individuals. Selecting and de-selecting the right people and making sure they are well trained is the easy bit, and the part that is most readily dealt with by throwing money at the problem. The magic comes when the team is instilled with self belief, energy, and determination to win.

If your strategy relies entirely on you personally – your constant presence, permanent smile, steady flow of jokes, anecdotes and advice – then it will fall down whenever you run out of steam. Presumably you have off days? Problems at home? Pressure from your boss? You need your team to be firing on all cylinders on those days too.

Motivation isn't really something you can "do" to someone. It comes from within the individual. The sales manager's role is to help people to become self-motivated so that they can perform well even when they're not being cajoled or encouraged.

Incentives and conditions

You can't coerce people to become motivated, but you can create a set of conditions in which motivation will bloom, and you can make incentives available that will motivate people to behave in the way you want them to.

Conditions are the things that are continually or frequently present – such as an overall sense of fun or excitement, camaraderie, sense of purpose, sense of urgency.

Incentives are those things that are held out as rewards for behaviour or achievement. People usually think of money and perks when they hear the word "incentive", and those are, of course, powerful incentives for salespeople. Money alone won't normally do it, though (and that can be an expensive lesson to learn!). In any sales team, a range of different incentives will influence different people in different measure, and we are all motivated by a combination of incentives rather than just one.

Your motivational levers

Some people say that the two big motivators are fear and greed. We'll unpack that slightly and broaden it out to include status and job satisfaction. We would also suggest that it is security – the reduction of fear – that is the incentive. Fear is what we're seeking to escape from.

Material reward	Job satisfaction	Status	Security

If we think of each type of incentive as a lever you can pull to help motivate your salespeople, then the four main levers are *material reward* (money, perks, prizes), *job satisfaction* (enjoying what you spend your time doing), *status* (having your worth acknowledged by your boss, yourself and those around you), and *security* (the reduction of fear and avoidance of negative things).

For something to act as an incentive it has to have certain properties. It has to be:

- **Relevant** to the person and the task
- **Desirable** to the recipient
- **Proportionate** to the challenge
- **Achievable** by the person to whom it is offered.

The prize money for winning the men's singles at Wimbledon this year is £1,000,000. It is double what it was 10 years ago and 50 times what it was 30 years ago.

£1,000,000 would be pretty desirable – enough to change our lives – but none of us in the Karlssen office are planning to make any effort at all to win Wimbledon this year, or any year. Unless you've got a hope of winning you're unlikely to be motivated towards the incentive.

For professional tennis players the money is relevant (they have a lifestyle to maintain), desirable (it's a million pounds), and proportionate (for the top players it is about 25% to 30% of their annual earnings)

But for the players who stand a realistic chance of winning it is probably not the principal incentive, but one of several incentives. There is also the status of joining an elite group within their chosen field, the ripple effect of product endorsements and TV contracts, and the incentive of celebrity. Tennis players tend to agree that Wimbledon is the one they most want to win. And yet, it is not the highest paid tournament by a long way. Take all the other incentives away and it would just be another tennis competition.

Material reward

Commission, bonus payments, stock options, company cars, and special perks are the meat and drink of sales management and probably have been since caveman days, when the Cave Manager first sent the Cave Executive out to barter for a carcass of beef.

Most companies are well aware of the potency of commission and bonus schemes for sales team motivation and the pool of money made available for incentives often represents a substantial financial investment.

But if you are not maximising the motivational impact of these schemes your money is probably being wasted.

Too many schemes are active demotivators, and often they encourage behaviour that's contrary to the interests of the company. Your incentive fund should work for you, not against you!

For financial and other material incentives to work well they should be should be short-term, simple, certain and achievable.

The Karlssen Standard
for reward schemes

Short term ✔	**Simple** ✔
Certain ✔	**Achievable** ✔

Short term

There is a large body of research to show that distant and uncertain long term rewards are nowhere near as motivating as imminent short-term rewards. This is true even if the long term rewards are huge and the short-term rewards are fairly small.

Think about the concentration and buzz in the office when sales people are trying to hit an end-of-the week target. Contrast this with the lack of energy around the far-off annual bonus.

Simple

Reward schemes should be so simple that salespeople can work out on their fingers how much money they will be taking home at the end of the month.

If I can see a tangible prize for making an extra call, closing an extra deal, then I'll do it. If on the other hand, I have a vague notion that lots of hard work and brilliance might pay off if a number of variables are aligned, then to be honest I might go and make myself a coffee.

Complex reward schemes backfire when salespeople cannot use them to keep constant score of their progress. If they require managers to work them out at the end of the month they lose motivational impact.

Certain

Think how enjoyable the weekend is after you've worked hard for five days and secured concrete results. You relax, recuperate, and enjoy yourself. On Monday you're refreshed and ready to repeat the experience. It's a positive, self-reinforcing cycle.

People feel good about work when they're clear about what success entails and how to achieve it. In many careers, success is a difficult concept to pin down, but in sales it's pretty simple. Many sales managers spoil it by failing to capitalise on the motivational boost that comes with clear, unambiguous success.

Uncertain targets and shifting goalposts are obvious motivation killers, but so are some of the most common reward schemes.

For instance, if individual rewards are only payable when the team or company as a whole hits certain targets, they lose impact. Schemes of this kind are tempting because they help mitigate risk and (in theory) encourage staff to be more team spirited. The most likely outcome, however, is that your best performers become disillusioned with the company and resentful of their teams. When a sales person closes a deal or hits a target you want that person to feel a surge of joy. Anticipation of that pleasure is something that will help get the salesperson up in the morning, and driven towards the next successful event. Why dampen that by adding an element of uncertainty?

If I need to close five deals to pay for a holiday, that's motivating. If five deals might-or-might not pay for my holiday depending on factors beyond my control, then I'm just a bit anxious.

Achievable

Incentive schemes should be stretching and challenging. They are the reward for achievement over and above the call of duty. But if an incentive scheme isn't achievable there's simply no point in having it. It loses its ability to motivate as soon as people realise they will never get their hands on the prize, and at that point becomes the focus of resentment.

Your sales team's targets should be achievable, even if yours aren't

If you work for a corporation, there's every chance your targets have become unachievable even before the financial year has commenced. You might or might not be willing to accept this for yourself, but you shouldn't let it drag down the performance of your sales team.

A typical top-down approach to target-setting has the company working out how much profit it wants to see next financial year and targeting each part of the business to achieve a certain amount of revenue. This requirement is divided between sales teams and then subdivided between sales people.

If all goes well, this division represents a realistic target for you and your team, and once you have implemented some strategic and process improvements, introduced better training and development and built a high-energy, motivated sales environment, you'll be able to hit the numbers.

But if it's just plain unachievable, you should move heaven and earth to avoid using targets you know cannot be reached as the benchmark for individual success by members of your team.

By unachievable we don't mean stretching, we mean targets you know your team will be unable to achieve. A sales team should be given targets that stretch and challenge them. But if they are unachievable they will simply lose their purpose and become demotivators.

If you can pitch for more resources to make the task a realistic one, then great. If not, you will either need to amend the target, or devise a way of rewarding the team for strong performance even if they fail to meet the target set at corporate level. The alternative is falling sales and an even bigger revenue gap.

Go easy on the basic salary

For sales people whose results are easy to measure we would recommend that you offer a generous, achievable and reliable commission scheme and that you keep basic salaries as low as you can.

A high basic salary can act as a disincentive, especially if it inhibits your ability to offer a really attractive commission scheme. When the guaranteed income is so high that the performance related component can be treated as icing on the cake, there's a much greater risk of complacency.

Dare you break the curse of the time-bound reward scheme?

It is rare to find a reward scheme that isn't tied to a monthly, quarterly, or annual cycle. A typical scheme involves a monthly sales target, and rewards salespeople who exceed that target.

The problem with that system, as you know, is that it encourages strange and counterproductive behaviour. Salespeople who realise midway through the month that they're not going to hit their targets are disinclined to close deals, preferring to drag their feet so that the sale counts towards the next month's result. Do you really want your people to slow down at certain times of the week, month or year? Your earnings and cash flow are deferred and, by failing to strike while the iron is hot, you lose a proportion of those sales.

At Karlssen we reward salespeople for each sale, and every fifth sale is rewarded double. It doesn't matter when that fifth sale is achieved. This means that our people are continually racing to meet the next target, and that target is always within relatively easy reach. Whether it happens on the Friday or the following Monday is unimportant. The blood doesn't start pumping on the last day of the month; it's pumping all the time.

Filling the incentive vacuum

The *incentive value* of a reward scheme is its power to incentivise you. For instance a stretching but achievable scheme with an imminent deadline and large potential payout has a high incentive value.

Let's imagine you are incentivised on an annual basis running from April to March.

When you start the year your target looks pretty easy. You're motivated to achieve it but there's no compelling need to work too hard, so at this stage your reward scheme has a moderate *incentive value*. It's enough to push you, but not to push you very hard.

Imagine that after your easy start to the year a seemingly red-hot prospect goes bust in May so you have a poor month, and during June and July one of your star salespeople is off work with a torn ligament. Your target now looks stretching and you're working doubly hard to try and meet it. The incentive value of your reward scheme has now become higher. A manageable but challenging target has a higher incentive value than an easy target because it forces you to work better and harder to achieve it.

But by September you're starting to wonder whether this year is actually a write-off and by October your target has become logically impossible to achieve. This is the point at which the incentive disappears, leaving a vacuum. The incentive value of your reward scheme has dropped to zero.

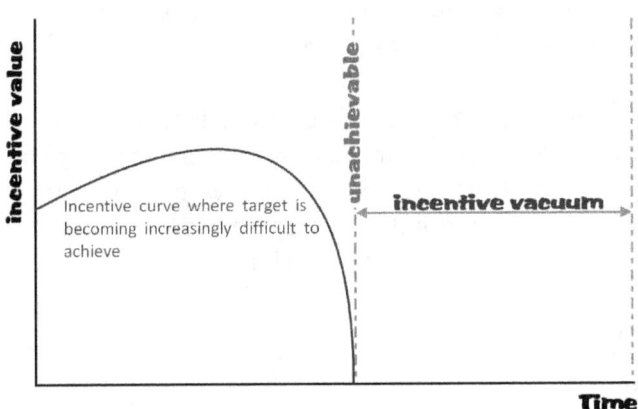

The bigger the vacuum, the longer the period that has to be filled by other incentives. If the only incentive to work hard is to hang onto your job that may work for a while, but sooner or later you can just find employment elsewhere.

Motivation isn't about crime and punishment. Yes, your good-for-nothing sales team will need a kick up the posterior if they fail to hit their targets, but your main problem isn't "how do I punish them" it's "how do I get them working" and the absence of financial incentive isn't going to help you there.

Short term schemes have an advantage in that there is more opportunity to start afresh. But remove the time-bound element completely and the vacuum disappears altogether.

A guaranteed reward is no incentive

The incentive vacuum can also apply to sales teams where excessive pampering takes place.

You've always got to have stretch for an incentive scheme to motivate. When targets are so easy they are certain to be achieved, the effect is to neuter the reward scheme. It becomes nothing more than a supplement to the basic salary and has no power to influence performance.

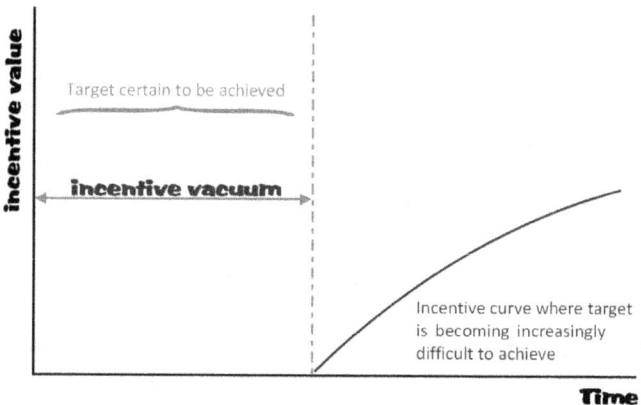

Don't let the incentive vacuum suck the oxygen from peak performance

We once worked for a client who set a target for his telephone team of 40 calls per day. The average number of calls for that team was 40 calls. Not 41 or 42, it was exactly 40. We suggested they could do better, so he increased the target to 60 calls and the average increased to exactly 60.

A similar thing can happen when people hit their sales target for the month. There's suddenly no financial incentive to keep going, so people do tend to slow down and even stop, conserving their energy or building up a pipeline for the next period. This is a waste. When people are on a roll they are capable of great things and the effective sales manager will capitalise on that.

Why not work a system where uncapped achievement is met by uncapped reward? Even better, why not reward extreme performance with extreme remuneration?

Job satisfaction

Are people who love their work more self-motivated?

Looking around at the people who do well, the evidence seems to speak for itself. Those who are truly outstanding are the ones with a passion for what they do. We spend much of our lives working, so enjoying work is important to anyone with a measure of choice about how they spend their time.

There are three main ways you can leverage job satisfaction to help your team become motivated:
1) By allocating work intelligently
2) By using enjoyable work as an incentive
3) By making your workplace fantastic

Allocate work intelligently

Of course there are constraints on your ability to reorganise peoples' work and responsibilities, but it is nevertheless something that can be done to some extent in almost any situation.

In your sales team, for instance, you might have a mix of "hunters" and "farmers". People who love going out and meeting new people, persuading, negotiating and closing deals are likely to be more motivated if they are focused mainly on new business development. Such people sometimes regard customer retention as dull and monotonous. People with "farmer" personalities, on the other hand, prefer building strong relationships with customers, looking after them, developing a deeper understanding of their needs, and making sure they're getting the best possible experience. If you have people on your team who are clearly farmers or clearly hunters, consider reallocating your new business and retention responsibilities accordingly.

In the same way there are some people who are temperamentally suited to key accounts, international travel, or telephone work whilst others are suited to small high volume sales, networking, social media or writing applications to tender. If you get people doing the work that suits them, they will be happier and more self motivated.

At Karlssen we often work with salespeople who love meeting clients, pitching and winning business, but dislike cold calling. We take on the cold calling part of the process, a burden is lifted from their shoulders, and they spend most of their working week on tasks they enjoy.

Make the workplace a bit more like prison

The most obvious example of the use of enjoyable work as an incentive is in prison, where the best behaved prisoners are rewarded with jobs in the garden or kitchen. Most of us try to make our offices as un-prisonlike as possible, but this might be something we can emulate.

If there is work that can be used to incentivise and reward high-performing team members, then why not make the most of it? It might be a trip to a popular conference with great leads, a sought after sales territory, or involvement in an exciting project. If you're transparent about how you plan to use such things as incentives for strong performance, and clear about the criteria for winning, then there's no reason why work can't in itself be the reward.

Make it a bit more like Mars

Creating a "fun" working environment is the trickiest thing to do deliberately. Nothing grates like enforced jollity. But it can be done, and it can be done well. After all, we do it all the time in our social lives. Fun doesn't tend to just happen; we make it happen by systematically organising parties and barbecues, sporting events, evenings out, weekend trips and holidays.

If you ever speak to someone who works at Mars, the UK confectionery company, ask them whether it's a fun place to work and they will probably tell you that it is. It's not just because of all the free chocolate, it's because the company has habits and traditions that are genuinely amusing and engaging. One person we know won a week's worth of packed lunches that had to be made for him each morning by his boss. Each day he looked forward to finding out which sandwich fillings his boss had chosen and what he'd put in for dessert. It was a small thing that was hugely inexpensive and easy-to-implement, but quirky, funny and memorable.

Another acquaintance worried that it might be prudent for her to move away from her current employer to gain broader experience. But she can't imagine that working anywhere else could be anything like as much fun. Her company was founded ten years ago and has grown into a multinational corporation turning over millions of pounds and employing 800 people. It is perhaps no coincidence that the management team have made time to devise all manner of amusing workplace activities including company sponsored ice creams on hot days, football screenings, and Friday afternoon drinks receptions where staff members do presentations to each other, sharing ideas and experience.

James Caan[1], the millionaire investor famous for his role in the BBC programme Dragons Den, made his money by founding and running a recruitment consultancy. He introduced a regular slot during office hours dedicated to having fun. He asked his people to devise the activities, and they became more and more imaginative as time went on, including karaoke and an office version of Blind Date.

---

[1] James Caan, The Real Deal, Virgin Books, 2009

Google is famous for being innovative in the way it helps motivate and retain its people. It offers onsite services to make life easier (dry-cleaning, massage) and when Google staff have new addition to their families Google picks up the tab on takeout meals for the first few weeks after the newborn arrives. Google also allows people to spend 20% of their office time on projects of their own choosing. This hasn't just made Google feel like a great place to work; it has unleashed creativity and led directly to the creation of new services including Gmail and Google News.

The marketing guru Seth Godin says that successful companies often give their customers something analogous to the free prize inside the cereal box – something quirky that distinguishes their product from its rivals. Consider taking the same approach to staff motivation. Sometimes it isn't the £3000 sales commission that really makes the difference, sometimes it's that you're looking forward to the vicars and tarts fancy dress softball competition.

Team spirit

Many salespeople are extroverts and enjoy being part of a team. The advantage for you is that teamwork helps raise energy levels and increases the help and support available to each team member.

There are a few things you can do to help foster a sense of team spirit. Most involve putting dates in your calendar.

- Don't assume the team will naturally gel. Take responsibility for making it happen. Create opportunities for them to interact – especially around work related matters.
- Set aside a regular slot in the diary for a team meeting. The purpose of this meeting isn't to bore everyone by going through each person's key performance indicators or sales pipeline (this is better done one-to-one or in very small groups). It's to discuss ideas, plans, best practice, the market, and whatever else is important. The idea is for everyone to contribute – not for you to deliver long lectures
- One idea that has worked well for us is to give each team member a subject to present at a team meeting (for instance analysis of a competitor or a market sector). People are allocated their presentation topics well in advance (ideally a schedule will be drawn up covering the following three months), giving each person plenty of time to prepare. One person presents at each meeting, followed by questions and discussion, and the meeting then moves on to the main agenda.
- Use a large white board to keep a record of everybody's live prospects and key performance indicators. This encourages people to take an interest in each others' progress and can foster a sense of healthy competition.
- Schedule in some extra-curricular activities. These might be trips to a restaurant, bar, theatre, bowling alley, or whatever seems appropriate. The trick is to get them in the diary rather than just talking about them. Put somebody in charge of arranging each outing and chase them up in the same way you would if it were any other project.

Mix things up

Make it interesting and glamorous to work for you. Use non-standard rewards when people overachieve. A meal for two or theatre tickets, for instance, enable your team members to share their success with partners or friends, and provide an excuse for them to talk about the achievement that led to the reward. Try using "red letter days" such as hot air ballooning, bungee jumping, a day in a Ferrari, a weekend at a spa. These are the sort of things that will get talked about within the company and beyond.

Status

Remember the awe you felt, on your first day as junior assistant to the assistant post room assistant, when you walked into that cavernous corner office occupied by the Chief Operating Officer, with its leather settee and walnut meeting table?

Remember the quiet pride when your boss confided in you about a major development that was still top secret and not to be discussed with other members of staff?

Remember when you were promoted to Sales Director and people just somehow started treating you better?

There are a number of ways to pull the "status lever". The important thing is to use it, and to try and be fair, consistent and strategic in the way you use it.

Status is a public thing and a private thing. In the same way that animals will fight for dominance within their own groups, people still seem to have a visceral need to clarify their positions in the pecking order. But it's also about self esteem. Even if it's never mentioned in public, the fact that your boss asks your opinion and tells you that you're the most commercially astute member of the team means a lot to you.

Recognition and praise

Many people say that recognition is more important to them than almost anything else. It goes without saying that praise is an incentive to succeed. When we're engaged in an important piece of work many of us are subconsciously imagining the reaction we'll get from the people we respect.

The value of praise, however, is not so much in the words, but in the fact that it's articulating something you feel. People want their managers to respect them, approve of them, and admire their work. Praise is the expression of that. It needs, therefore, to be authentic. Your body language and manner of delivery are important too. "Nice work" delivered with a warm and genuine smile can have a lot more impact than gushing tributes that aren't quite believable. Praise loses its value (and the person offering it loses credibility) if it is given excessively, glibly, lazily or wrongly.

When you praise something it's worth explaining why. Describe what you liked about it and the impact it had. "I liked the way you handled that objection" is fine, but it might leave the recipient wondering why. It helps to elaborate: "I liked the way you handled that objection because you managed to get the customer to answer her own question, and I think that was a big part of the reason you closed the sale".

If something is especially praiseworthy then repeat the praise later to reinforce it. For instance, if somebody excels in a sales appointment or writes a great tender document it's a good idea to praise them immediately, but then praise them again in a more formal environment – at a team meeting or during an appraisal.

It's easy to publicly recognise your out-and-out stars (and you should do so) but since you want your middle ranking players to be motivated too it's also appropriate to praise people who aren't the usual suspects. It's important that the praise is legitimate and deserving, and given in the appropriate context. It's also important to explain why you're giving the praise so that it doesn't come across as glib. "I think we should all give a round of applause to Jane Smith who seems to be a whizz with that thing on the computer where you store all that customer information" doesn't work as well, for instance, as "Please make sure you make complete notes in the contact management system because it's so easy to forget a lot of the detail if you don't. If you look at the notes Jane Smith makes you'll see a perfect example of how to do it well."

Ownership

Ameera wasn't the most diligent student in the world and was unceremoniously booted out of college after her first year. She was her parents' pride and joy and had never really had to work very hard for anything. She did a bit of temping, but couldn't stand the boredom. She got a job at a law firm as an office junior but felt increasingly claustrophobic.

Then one day in September a close friend wangled her a job at a branch of Waterstone's Booksellers. She was given the Finance, Economics and Law section to look after. Waterstone's at that time had a very particular management style. New recruits were immediately thrown in at the deep end. Ameera was a hundred percent responsible for her part of the shop. It was her job to make sure the shelves were stocked, and that old books were returned to the publisher. She had to keep the place tidy, work the till, help customers find the right books and make sure the stocklist remained current and relevant.

Within a few days she was in love with her job. The pay was terrible, customers were demanding, and her brother called her "shop girl" but she just didn't stop smiling. She would stay behind after hours to restock shelves and get in early to place orders with publishing companies. Within three years she was running her own branch and now runs a chain of wholefood stores.

If you've ever been allocated tasks piecemeal you'll know how disempowering it can be. It makes you feel subservient, like you've been co-opted to do someone else's work. It's also less interesting to do a piece of work if you can't see the big picture and don't have authority to make tactical decisions.

If you're given overall charge of something however, whether it's a particular market or territory, a report, project, process, or area of work, you feel a sense of ownership. The thing won't happen unless you make it happen. You'll take the blame if it goes badly and the credit if it works well. That's a tremendously motivating feeling.

Career advancement

It's pretty rare to get to the end of a job interview with a prospective salesperson without being asked "What are the opportunities for promotion at this company?" and it's not unusual for team members to ask when they can expect to be promoted to the next stage.

The pay rise is an important part of it, but you're missing a trick if you over employ pay rises and under employ the use of formal promotions.

Promotion is an invaluable tool for employers, because it offers a visible measure of overall worth and success. Your job title is one of the ways in which you are labelled and evaluated at work and by the community at large. A promotion is something you are expected to tell your partner and family about, whereas bonus payments and praise are harder to crowbar into the conversation.

However flat your hierarchy is, and irrespective of whether you need your team members to do essentially the same work as one another, it is wise to develop a clear system for career advancement which visibly and indelibly recognises individuals for the progress they have made. Ideally it will include a number of steps (Sales Assistant, Sales Executive, Account Manager, Account Director for instance), and ideally each step will carry with it additional responsibility together with additional privileges.

Whereas people sometimes resent jobs that are distributed ad-hoc or lumped onto an existing workload, if you formalise the addition of responsibilities and make them a consequence of promotion they are normally welcomed.

As talented people become more experienced they want to take on greater challenges, be given more responsibility, and learn more. These are incentives because they increase job satisfaction and prepare the recipient for bigger promotions yet to come.

Promotions don't need to include line management

Good salespeople often get undone by having people report to them, and this can be demotivating for all concerned. Even a single line report is a major disruption to someone who has not managed people before and whose routine can't really accommodate it. Management is a time consuming job, and it works best when you have fewer managers and allow them to dedicate serious time to the business of management.

Security

For some, security is a strong incentive. It motivates us to buy insurance, pay into pension funds, marry the dull but nice boy rather than the attractive but dangerous one. At work it can also be a powerful incentive, spurring us to work harder and develop skills so that we might safeguard our position, guard against redundancy, fend off competition.

The need for security is essentially a reaction against fear. Fear is a famously powerful leadership tool, and has been used to great effect by many of the best known leaders from Attila the Hun to "Neutron" Jack Welch (who, as we will discuss later, insisted that the lowest performing 10% should be sacked each year).

The extent to which you use fear as a motivational lever will depend partly on your personality and values, partly on the culture in which you operate, and partly on the individuals with whom you work. But the chances are you will use fear to some extent because at times the avoidance of negative outcomes is a strong incentive for people to act. You will probably use a combination of "carrot" and "stick" in the way you manage people day to day.

Fear can be used to jog people out of their complacency, create a sense of urgency, or to force people to adapt to changing circumstances. A popular technique for introducing radical change into an organisation is "the burning platform", in which people are told that if the company doesn't make significant changes it will be engulfed by catastrophe.

The psychologist Neil Fiore[2] invites readers to imagine they are asked to walk on a board thirty feet long and one foot wide. It's an easy thing to do. But imagine the board is suspended between two buildings 100 feet above the pavement. In that context it becomes a daunting idea, does it not?

Now imagine that you suddenly hear the crackling noise of fire, feel immense heat on your back and turn round to see flames enveloping the building you are standing on. Suddenly the focus has changed from the fear of walking on the board to the greater fear of not doing so.

The important thing to remember about fear is that it can be used to generate urgent, short term activity but can't be used to drive long term behaviour. The evacuation of Dunkirk was possible because the emergency was acute and the goal was immediate. If people live in a constant state of anxiety and fear, however, their morale begins to drop and they become less productive. A presiding culture of fear is inconsistent with job satisfaction.

---

[2] Neil Fiore, Ph.D., The now habit: A strategic programme for overcoming procrastination, Penguin, 2007

THE MOTIVATING SALES MANAGER

Getting it done

The obvious and reasonable retort is that there simply aren't enough hours in the day to look at each of your team members in turn and devise tailor made motivation strategies for each of them. This is true, so here are some ways in which you can develop a range of incentives for your team that will have maximum impact with manageable effort.

Focus most on your "middle 70%"

Jack Welch rose within General Electric to become its CEO and held that position for 20 years. During his tenure the company's market capitalisation grew from $13 billion to $400 billion, making him one of the most successful corporate executives in history.

Probably his best-known management model is the 20, 70, 10 rule[3]. It is controversial because he argues that the weakest 10% of your staff should be sacked every year. But the important message is actually this:

20,70,10	Your results will be strongest if you focus not on your stars (the best performing 20%) or your laggards (the worst performing 10%), but on the 70% of people in the middle. Think hardest about what you need to do to motivate this middle 70%

---

[3] Jack Welch, Winning, HarperTorch, 2007

Whether or not you agree with Welch's trigger-happy approach towards low-achievers, his advice regarding the middle 70% is sound.

The stars and the laggards are much more likely to be on your radar. When you think about "the team" which individuals do you think of first? When you imagine pitching an idea to them, which audience members appear in sharpest focus?

But when it comes to getting the biggest bang from your leadership buck, it's the people in the middle who count. Your high-flyers will by nature be bright and self-motivated. Recognise them and reward them generously, listen to them, support them, and let them get on with it. Your weakest 10% can occupy a huge amount of time and energy. With a lot of effort you can turn them round, but wouldn't that effort be better directed at the rest of the team?

The biggest impact will be achieved by focusing on your unremarkable majority. They are the most abundant in number and the most responsive to good leadership.

Pull each of the levers and people will self-select what motivates them

As long as you're pulling each of the levers – material reward, job satisfaction, status, security – and you're doing it in a planned and effective way, the various members of your team are likely to be incentivised by one or other of the incentives on offer. You might not have the capacity to tailor incentives to suit the personality of each member of the group, but you can offer a blend of incentives that appeal to most.

Your behaviour

Your behaviour as a leader will influence your team in a number of ways. Whether or not your people realise it, and whether or not you realise it, you're a role model. Your behaviour and attitude sets the tone and people will unconsciously mimic you (even if they neither like nor admire you). To an extent your thoughts, feelings and behaviour will be reflected back at you by your team. If you can motivate yourself (of which more later), you've got a much more chance of motivating your team.

You set the pace. If you expect things to be done quickly, and by pre-agreed times, then your people will act more quickly and pay closer attention to deadlines.

It's your job to inject energy into your team. You'll do this by interacting with them day-to-day, taking an interest in the small everyday details that are important to their success, noticing what they do, especially their achievements. If you're upbeat, positive, and happy that feeling will rub off on your people. If you are low-energy yourself you should do everything you can to address that. Eat more raw fruit and vegetables, get enough sleep, make sure you schedule-in plenty of life enhancing leisure activity (again, more of this later)

You're the person who signals to the team what the priorities are. If you are clear about what's important and how you want your people to behave, they'll feel a greater sense of certainty and be more purposeful about achieving your goals.

Have a plan

People feel much, much happier following someone who seems to know what they're doing. It's motivating to follow a competent person, because the chances of success seem higher. If you've ever been managed by an idiot, you'll know how demotivating that is.

If you're a competent leader, you'll have a plan. You won't just turn up and see what happens. When you organise meetings with your people, you'll have an agenda – even if it's just a six point note you scribbled for yourself before you entered the room.

Having a plan doesn't mean you know all the answers in advance, and the plan can change as circumstances change.

It's acceptable to tell your team that you don't have a plan yet, but you're working on it and will unveil it a week on Tuesday. At least you're planning to write a plan.

Your plan can be simple, and you don't need to devise it yourself. Your plan can initially be: "We're going to come up with a plan together".

But if you're reading this and thinking "actually, I don't have a plan" or "my team don't have the foggiest idea what the plan is", then in twenty pages time it'll be time to start planning.

Beat inertia

Inertia is the enemy of motivation. When people slow down, every little activity seems like a major effort. We once knew a salesperson whose days became so empty he eventually spent six out of every eight hours playing a children's game on the internet.

Keep your team moving, and working. Inactivity at work has the emotional impact of being in a traffic jam. It is more motivating to go the long way round than to sit still.

Make sure they understand you're serious

If it's important whether or not your team hit their daily call targets, close a certain number of deals, achieve a certain yield target, write carefully-crafted emails, adopt your favoured sales technique, then make sure they know that it matters very much to you. It might be nice to hang out in an office where the boss is laid back, but it's more motivating to be in a workplace where there's a clear sense of purpose and where it matters what you do and how you do it.

Remember people care more about themselves than they do about you

Though they would avoid saying so, people tend to be much more motivated by the prospect of personal gain – whether that be material, status, job satisfaction or security – than they are by any burning ambition on behalf of their company, department or boss. Are they going to get promoted or do they risk redundancy? How are they perceived by their manager and their peers? These things mean more to people than whether the company stays within the FTSE 250 or whether you hit your quarterly budget forecast.

You'll help people become motivated by addressing their personal ambitions and concerns and helping to resolve them favourably. If you can align their personal interests with the company's interests, then you're in business. You'll also make yourself more relevant to them and be better able to guide and influence their behaviour.

Give feedback effectively

Even hardened salespeople need feedback. They need reassurance and praise, and they need constructive criticism to help them develop and achieve more.

Do make time to listen in on calls, accompany people on sales visits, cast an eye over meeting notes, examine pipeline numbers, and discuss challenges and successes.

When a salesperson closes a particularly tricky or lucrative deal, ask him what he thinks he did right. Dwelling in detail on success is great for motivation because it lifts the spirits, gives people something positive to look back on at times of self-doubt, and helps people better understand how to be successful in future.

As for criticism, some may shy away from it because they fear it will be hard to take, but if it's delivered constructively it will be a relief to hear even if you're asking for improvements. People want to know where they stand and how they're doing.

Feedback should be offered frequently and without too much gravity. Don't bottle it up or wait for formal opportunities. It should be a natural part of your day-to-day interaction with people who depend on you for guidance.

Don't get emotional. If you feel frustrated, walk away and deal with the matter when you're able to do so calmly and constructively.

Criticism should focus on behaviour and technique rather than on the personality or qualities of the recipient. Phrases like "you're not very persuasive", "your telephone style is weak", "you're a bit lazy" are destructive rather than constructive because they suggest that the problem is intractable. You can use questions to encourage the person to come up with ideas himself ("You attended fewer appointments last month than most team members. What do you think you could do to fill up your diary?") or you can be more directive ("You are likely to have more success on the phone if you speak more slowly") – either way, criticism should address specific behaviour and encourage the recipient to work towards a solution.

Performance appraisals should never replace informal feedback, but they are essential because they provide people with a formal opportunity to raise issues that might bother them. However many times you lean on someone's desk and ask "How are things going?", there are some people who will always wait for their appraisal to really unburden themselves, and will feel increasingly anxious and bereft if that opportunity is denied to them.

Win a lot

People do better when they feel like they're winning. They're more confident, take more pleasure in their work, and are more positive towards each other and their customers.

Create opportunities for your team to win – by setting short term challenges that are stretching but achievable. The first element is the commission and bonus scheme, which, as we have discussed above, should systematically reward short-term achievements. You can also devise other challenges, maybe focusing on specific KPI's such as yield or retention. One team we know devised something called the "Curry Hurry" – as soon as the team hit a certain revenue level they would celebrate with a raucous night at the local Indian restaurant.

When people succeed, it's good to have little rituals in place to mark the occasion. Most sales teams use whiteboards and many ask people to post their successes on the board personally (whether that means booking a sales appointment or closing a deal). It's interesting that even hardened old timers tend to get a thrill from this.

Don't be a stool pigeon

A man we know called Tim spent some time as a teacher in Vietnam. Some way through his final term he realised his class of eight year olds could do with an extra incentive to excel in their end of year exam, so he promised that if they achieved a certain pass rate he would bring in some cakes and fizzy drinks and they would have a picnic.

The exams were duly taken and the class exceeded expectations. Everyone was delighted, but on the appointed day of the picnic, Tim's promise completely slipped his mind. His class of twenty Vietnamese eight year olds turned up to class, eyes twinkling expectantly, to be met only by the usual desks and exercise books, with Tim mapping out the day's lesson on the blackboard.

"Teacher Tim" said a boy sitting on the front row, struggling to keep his lower lip from wobbling, "you are a stool pigeon".

When Tim got home and looked the phrase up in the dictionary, he was suitably humbled.

Sadly for the eight year olds though, it was just an early lesson in what to expect from corporate life. Managers are always encouraging people to expect great things just over the horizon, whether they be pay rises, improved performance schemes, investment in sales support marketing, fairer distribution of territories, a better CRM system, involvement in sexy projects or a trip to Amsterdam. Too often, these promises evaporate, demoralising the team and weakening the incentive value of future promises.

The important thing is not to give up making promises, but to make them sparingly, only when you know you can deliver, and to always deliver on them. Even if you promise something small – a trip to the pub, say – you should follow through. When you turn out to be too busy on the day and the expected treat fails to materialise, you suck a bit of energy from your team.

Manage expectations. The truth is, there are always frustrations and not everything will be dealt with at once. Be realistic and honest. Encourage people to find their own solutions and work-arounds. Of course you should have a programme of improvements to benefit your team, but it will take time to deliver. Be realistic about the amount you are able to take on, specific about what you're planning to achieve and when it's likely to come to fruition, and then put a workable plan together to make it happen.

If team leadership needs to take second place, delegate it

There are all sorts of different things at work you might legitimately need to focus on if you are to succeed in your career. They might include, for instance, your involvement with corporate strategy, company politics, or being a player in the industry more widely. It might be that you're quietly staging a coup to replace the CEO, or you're leading a buyout of one of your competitors. These might be your top priorities, but some of them might have nothing to do with building a motivated sales team. Sometimes your people lose their energy because you happen to be distracted by things that don't directly affect them.

If you're too wrapped up in other things to focus on these two priorities, and you're committed to building or maintaining a motivated sales team, then you should delegate the leadership of the team to someone else – someone who will be obsessed with the success of the sales team and undistracted by the wider corporate agenda.

Delegating your sales leadership role means giving full ownership to someone else, and paring your personal involvement back to one of strategic oversight. You will continue to be responsible for the management and motivation for the sales leader, but will take a hands-off approach to the staff.

If you can't delegate, get your ducks in a row

If it's impossible to delegate your sales management responsibilities, the next best thing is to make sure you have rock solid systems in place to ensure the right incentives and conditions exist to keep your team motivated while you are distracted by other things.

That means, for instance, that your regular sales meetings are in the calendar and will take place whether you're present or not. If you're not present, the agenda should be clear enough for people to progress without you, it should be clear who will be chairing the meeting, who is responsible for taking notes, and how you want outcomes to be implemented and reported. It also means that somebody is tasked with making sure that commission is worked out and communicated at the right time, that social events and other get togethers happen and that the various rituals are obseved that keep the team's energy high and overcome inertia.

Self motivation

Physician heal thyself

To build a motivated sales team, you are at least going to have to put on a pretty good show of being motivated yourself.

Firstly you need to care about winning – which means you take real, obvious pleasure in success, and you address problems and obstacles with seriousness and vigour. Secondly you need to care about the things that matter – in this context that means they make a difference to the performance of your team.

To build a motivated sales team, there are two things you really need to care about:
- Hitting your sales goals
- The individual members of their team hitting their sales goals – especially those in the "middle 70%"

Get your mojo back

It happens to the best of us, sometimes when we least expect it. It might be that you've been doing the same job for too long and are bored, or it might be the opposite – you feel overwhelmed, or don't really believe you can succeed.

There are two big ways of dealing with this.
- Getting a life
- Getting organised

If your career matters to you and you feel you're not really doing enough at work, you punish yourself by denying yourself some of the nicer things in life, and in doing so you create a vicious circle.

For instance, lets say your morale is low and you've become a procrastinator. You know you should be organising that team away-day, joining the new guy on some sales meetings, taking a good look at your team's KPI's. But you can't be bothered. Instead you update your Facebook status and watch funny clips on You Tube.

You feel guilty about it and you hang around the office, maybe moving your monthly sales report around the plate with your fork. You go home a bit late and don't feel like doing anything productive or enjoyable in the evening, and the next day you repeat the cycle.

Your guilt and fatigue is preventing you from doing fun stuff, and the lack of fun stuff in your life is making you feel subconsciously resentful of work and is sapping your energy and drive.

The first step in breaking this cycle is actually by starting with the fun stuff rather than the work stuff.

Think about what you really enjoy doing that doesn't involve staying up all night or forcing bad things into your body. Don't think about what you should be doing, or what other people want you to do. Think about what you love spending time doing, and that makes you feel good and relaxed afterwards.

It might be sailing, or fishing, watching films, eating out, trainspotting, rock climbing, rugby, golf, making new friends, seeing old friends, visiting your Granny, trips to foreign cities, time on the sunbed, dancing, going out on dates, amateur dramatics, massage, lacrosse, poetry readings or marathon running.

Now get your calendar and the relevant contact phone numbers and emails, and schedule plenty of this into your diary. If your chosen activities are frankly a bit unaffordable, choose alternatives you can afford. But don't neglect this important stage in the process. You're not doing it because you're being self indulgent; you're doing it because we told you to.

Once your diary is packed with good stuff, you should start filling your diary with the things you need to do to succeed at work. Please don't jump directly to this second stage first. Start with the enjoyable leisure activities because they provide a framework for your life around which the hard work fits. They are the reward for effort and they are the the things that refresh and re-energise you.

Now look at what you need to do to achieve a motivated sales team. Schedule in some thinking and planning time and diarise the team meetings, the outings, the one-to-ones, and everything else.

When you've done that, think about the projects you find most daunting and difficult. For each task create a project plan, working back chronologically from the deadline, and list the tasks that need to be performed between now and then to meet all the deadlines in between. Divide and subdivide these tasks into smaller component parts, until you get to the point where (a) you feel you are able to cope or (b) you realise that they aren't do-able within the timeframe so you're going to have to either extend deadlines, sacrifice some of the lower-priority objectives, or parcel-up some of the project activities into decent sized chunks and delegate those jobs to other people

It might not look at first glance as though this is all about self-motivation, but self-motivation will be a natural by product of getting your house in order.

A final point. We are more self-motivated when we have an end in sight and a deadline to work to that's not too far in the future. That is one of the reasons why breaking projects down into pieces works, and why it helps to work backwards from your ultimate deadline to create a number of smaller deadlines. Your working life should be a combination of deadlines set by your project planning process, and deadlines that arise because you have something fun to do.

Fail your way to victory

Psychologist Neil Fiore[4] argues that the difference between winners and losers is that winners fail often, whereas losers fail only once.

---

[4] Neil Fiore, Ph.D., The now habit: A strategic programme for overcoming procrastination, Penguin, 2007

Winners have a greater tolerance of failure: they brush themselves down and start again. They take on new challenges, keep going even when it gets tough, and try again when it doesn't work out. As a result, they achieve things. "Losers" on the other hand, are easily put off and therefore fail less often, but also achieve less.

For his bestseller *Outliers*, Malcolm Gladwell[5] researched people at the extremes of success: musicians, sports stars, millionaire businesspeople. He found that one thing they had in common, and a defining feature of their success, was that they practised a lot. Not just a little bit more than most people, but a scale of magnitude more than most people. On average, 10,000 hours of practice is what it takes to become outstanding in your field. Practising is really just controlled failure. If you've ever learned an instrument you'll remember the early days of repeated squeaks and missed notes. You keep failing and failing and failing until you succeed.

Questioned about his failed attempts at invention, Thomas Edison famously said that he had not failed 1000 times; he had discovered 1000 ways not to do it, each time moving a step closer to success. Edison made a commercial breakthrough with his incandescent light bulb and founded General Electric, which remains one of the world's biggest companies to this day.

---

[5] Malcolm Gladwell, Outliers, 2009

Work through the dip

Will King[6] was made redundant in the early 1990's and decided he wanted to market an oil based shaving lubricant he had created himself for his sensitive skin. He designed a logo on his computer at home, maxed out his credit cards, arranged for some plastic bottles to be produced, and hand-filled 9,600 of them over the kitchen sink in a flat he shared with his girlfriend.

He then wrote to all the retailers and pharmacists he could find. No response. He called them. They wouldn't take his calls. He kept calling. He begged and pleaded to be given the chance to pitch. Months went by. Eventually a buyer for one of the major chains agreed to give him fifteen minutes. He spent days working up a presentation, developing display materials, refining his argument. The buyer took one look at his miniature bottle of shaving oil and told him to leave. It would never sell. He was wasting her time.

Having tried and failed with Boots and the other chain stores, King decided to target Harrods – a store that might be willing to give shelf space to a small independent brand. He managed to speak to the men's grooming buyer and wasn't dismissed out of hand, so he kept at it. "We were involved in discussions for months and annoyingly she wouldn't make a decision, and I was just burning up money: Mum and Dad's money, my money, and I couldn't understand why. I mean, what was the risk? The opening order was going to be about £2.50." Eventually he got so frustrated he called Mohammed

---

[6] Will King, How to Build a Great Business in Tough Times, Business Plus, 2009

Al Fayed's office directly and got through to his PA. He asked for Mr Fayed's fax number and faxed through an order, which was signed and returned to him the next day, and with that he was a Harrods supplier.

At first Harrods sold one bottle of King's shaving oil about every two weeks. His first year sales were £300. But he then managed to close deals with some more stockists and in his second year he made £58,000 revenue, though his losses were £70,000. The next year, having hooked up with a business partner and raised £100,000 through a government loan guarantee scheme, he made £1000 profit on £250,000 worth of sales. Two years later he was turning over £1.5 million. By 2012 his company, King of Shaves, is expected to turn over £200 million.

The Dip

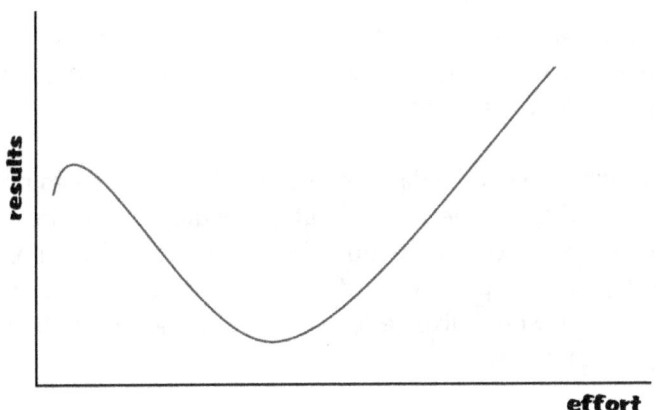

Marketing Guru and serial entrepreneur Seth Godin[7] says that almost everything in life worth doing is controlled by "the dip".

When you first start doing something it's fun. Expectations are still low, feedback is good, and you're enjoying the novelty of a new experience. Over the next few weeks you're learning a lot, and you're still full of energy and hope, and that keeps you going.

Then the dip happens.

The dip is the long slog between starting something and achieving mastery. During the dip you make false starts, get things wrong, bang your head against the wall trying to set up new processes, get projects going, build relationships. It's a lot of work for little or no reward.

The dip is what you face as a new salesperson or a new manager. You experience it when you join a new company or take on a new challenge.

It's tough being in the dip, but once you're in it keep going, because when you get up and out of the dip life becomes so much easier. Successful people don't just ride out the dip, they lean into it, pushing harder and changing the rules as they go. They don't like being in the dip so they work their way out of it.

---

[7] Seth Godin, The Dip, Piatkus, 2007

Once you're through the dip you've acquired skills, knowledge, a track record and a set of relationships that are hard to come by. The very fact that they were hard to come by – that you worked your way through a dip to get them – puts you at an advantage because the dip is a barrier to competition. Others will have attempted the dip and given up halfway through. Some will have contemplated it and decided not to bother. Once you're through the dip you will need to work less hard to achieve double the results.

Quit often and early

Godin makes another important point. Successful people are quitters. They quit often and early.

It's worthwhile struggling through the dip when the prize is worth working for. But don't be afraid of quitting if you realise the prize is too small, or if it is simply unreachable. Just make sure you work this out at an early stage, before you've spent time in the dip, and take decisive action.

If you try new things, many of them are likely to be duds. The trick is to be open minded, undefensive, and self-aware. Recognise bad ideas, excessive risk, and unachievable tasks for what they are at the earliest moment and get out. Save your blood sweat and tears for the challenges that can be overcome and for those where the prize is big enough to justify your effort.

Your big potatoes and your peanuts

Being overwhelmed at work; having things hanging over you; not feeling you've got the important things done; having to work late in the office over and over again; having your freedom restricted by the arrival of urgent deadlines; never having time to catch up. These are motivation killers. Get on top of them and you'll feel much better able to tackle things with energy and enjoy your work.

In *Cold Calling for Chickens*, sales guru Bob Etherington[8] describes a presentation he likes to give on the subject of time management.

He puts a large jar on the table in front of him. Then he reaches into his bag and grabs several big baking potatoes, which he places into the jar, asking the audience to tell him when he has filled it up. Once the potatoes have reached the top of the jar, the audience tend to call out that the jar is full.

"Ah!" exclaims Etherngton, "But is it?". He then grabs a bag of peanuts and begins feeding them into the holes left between the potatoes. When he has filled every hole he can find, he produces first a bag of chick peas and then a bag of lentils. Once the lentils have been fed into the jar, the audience is generally happy that the jar is indeed filled to capacity. At which point Etherington brings out a bag of sugar and pours it into the jar, filling the remaining gaps.

---

[8] Bob Etherington, Cold Calling for Chickens, Marshall Cavendish, 2006

He then asks the audience how they think the exercise relates to time management, and is rewarded by a number of suggestions along the same lines – that there's always scope to fit a bit more into the time available.

"Oh no, that's not it at all" says Bob. "The point is that if you don't put the big potatoes in first, you'll never fit them in at all."

There are a million things that can fill your day if you let them. If you want to be effective you will simply have to sacrifice some of them. The important thing is to avoid sacrificing the big potatoes – the things that really determine whether you succeed. If you're a sales manager, big potatoes include making sure your team know what they're supposed to be doing, how to do it, and what the rewards are. If you're a sales person, the big potatoes include developing leads, meeting prospects, closing deals, and making sure that contracts and invoices are dealt with. The only way to ensure that your "Priority One" tasks are completed is to do them first. Leave the peanuts and the lentils till later.

Complete your high leverage activities first

A time management technique that works brilliantly involves dividing your tasks between "high leverage" and "low leverage" activities.

High leverage activities are those that set in train a series of events that you don't necessarily need to be involved with yourself. Often they are activities where you personally are a bottleneck in the process. Once you've done your bit, other people can do their bit.

For instance, training your team to sell the newly launched product is a high leverage activity. Once you've done it, your team will go away and be busily productive. Commissioning an agency to develop a website for you would be another example. Once you've given them the brief, they are empowered to become busy on your behalf.

It's called "high leverage" because the amount of work achieved is high in proportion to the amount of energy you personally expend.

Low leverage activities are those that require you to work at something on your own, without it resulting in other work being done by others.

The earlier you get your high leverage activities completed, the more you will achieve over a given time period. If your high leverage stuff is completed on Monday, then other people have the rest of the week to finish off what you have started. You will be simultaneously free to complete your low leverage activities.

Positive thinking and the river of excrement

Gavin Aubrey, a sales motivation expert and owner of training company Think, uses a vivid metaphor to help people to think more positively[9]. Everyone, he says, has a river of excrement running under their lives. When things are going well you hardly notice it's there, but when things are going badly you do notice it's there and you take a good bathe in it.

It doesn't matter who you are; everyone has a river of excrement. The world can be a pretty brutal place and life isn't fair. Many of our problems are caused by sheer bad luck or by other people.

But it's your choice whether or not you let it suck you in. The happiest and most effective people are those who find ways of spending as much time as possible reflecting on positive things and as little time as possible dwelling on negative things.

Aubrey suggests six simple steps for getting out and staying out of the river of excrement:

Step 1 – *Activate your environment*: If things aren't going well, do something different. If you're in a bad mood, lacking energy, feeling anxious, then stand away from what you're doing, maybe go for a walk, get some fresh air, bark like a dog, anything to change your thought patterns.

---

[9] Gavin Aubrey, The River of Poo, MP3, Think Training, www.thinktd.co.uk

Step 2 - *Control your environment*: "If you lie down with dogs you get fleas". If you spend lots of time listening to people who do lots of moaning and groaning it will bring you down. Spend time with people who lift you and give you energy. If you work better with a tidy desk then tidy it. If fresh flowers raise your spirits, then fill your office with them. Do everything you can to increase the positive energy around you.

Step 3 – *What you think is what you are*: If you think of yourself as a loser you'll be a loser; if you think about how to succeed, you'll succeed. It all depends on the questions you ask yourself. If you ask "why did that go wrong" the answer might be "because I'm an idiot", but if you ask yourself "how could that have gone better" then you've learned something and you're better equipped for next time. The trick is to keep asking better questions and keep finding better solutions.

Step 4 – *Future thinking* – Most peoples' lives are ruled by their subconscious. By visualising the outcome you want, you're training your subconscious to accept that outcome as reality and act towards it. For instance, if you've ever purchased a house you'll remember the point where you started thinking about yourself in that house, picturing yourself at the breakfast table, perhaps, or imagining how you'd furnish certain rooms. By doing so, you were creating the right conditions to start engaging with the practical steps involved in buying the house.

You can deliberately activate future thinking by taking a few moments of quiet time and visualising the outcome you want. By doing so you will make that outcome more likely Step 5 – *Access states of excellence*: Your past life will have been filled with good times and bad times. These memories are buried deep in your subconscious but can be easily accessed, for instance by a particular smell or a song. They are also a bit like a juke box. You can play memories like tunes and they will each evoke a different reaction.

If you think about some of the bad times, times you behaved like an idiot, or times when other people did you wrong, then your mood and your self-image will start deteriorating. If, on the other hand, you want to feel positive or confident, then reflect on a time you felt confident or positive. Remember what you saw, felt, or heard. When people think about things that haven't gone so well they become depressed, but when you think about things you've done well you become energised.

Step 6 – *Have a positive brainwash*: Choose a day (perhaps today?) and whatever fate has in store for you on that day, turn it into a positive. Do the same the next day. The longer you can keep it up the better, but you don't need to do it for ever. You're training your mind to think positively, and that makes it easier to think positively in future.

Help others become self motivated

The above points apply to your people too, and talking them through with your team members will help you to motivate your people in two ways: Firstly you'll help them develop practical techniques; secondly you'll make them feel that they have a boss who adds real value and who cares about helping them perform rather than simply hectoring them about performance.

The winning attitude

Motivation is the fuel for success. Your responsibility as the leader of salespeople is to pull the right levers and create the conditions that allow self-motivation to flourish. You do so by creating incentives. Some people are motivated by material reward, some by job satisfaction, some by status, some by the need for security, and most of us are motivated by a combination of all of these.

If you create the right conditions and incentives, your people will become motivated, in different ways and for different reasons, by various parts of the motivational blend you have developed.

If you can organise yourself to implement a framework and set of incentives for your people, and motivate yourself to make it work, the chances are you will have a happy, productive and market beating team.

A small boy of our acquaintance was auditioning with his classmates for a school play. His mother knew that he had set his heart on being in the play, but the competition was stiff. Almost every other child in the class was auditioning too. She feared he would react badly if he was not chosen, and a lollipop was at the ready to ease the pain. On the day the parts were awarded, the boy's mother congregated with the other parents around the school gate to collect her son. As soon as the school doors opened the little boy leapt out and rushed up to her, eyes shining with pride and excitement. "Guess what Mum," he shouted, "I've been chosen to clap and cheer."

Checklist

Material reward

Are your reward schemes:

* Simple
* Certain
* Achievable
* Short term?

Job satisfaction

Do you:

* Allocate work intelligently?
* Use enjoyable work as an incentive?
* Make your workplace fantastic?

Status

Do you:

* Recognise each team member, not just the stars?
* Use praise effectively and authentically?
* Give ownership?
* Offer a clear career structure?
* Set out what people need to do to progress?
* Set out what responsibilities people will gain?

Security

Do you:

* Provide honest appraisal of the risks of failure?
* Use fear only when appropriate – to galvanise people to overcome short term problems?
* Resist developing a culture of fear

Checklist

Your behaviour	Job satisfaction
Do you:	Do you:
* Have a plan?	* Focus on the things that matter for team motivation?
* Work against inertia – keep your team moving?	
* Make it clear you're serious about winning?	* Properly delegate team leadership when you can't focus on it yourself
* Make it clear you're serious about the performance of each team member?	* Have systems in place to keep things working if you can't delegate leadership?
* Give feedback effectively?	* Schedule things you love doing into your leisure time?
* Take responsibility for team spirit?	* Organise your work time effectively and plan projects in advance?
* Mix things up and keep it interesting?	* Fail frequently and keep at it?
* Create opportunities for people to "win" and celebrate success?	* Work through the dip when the prize justifies it?
* Remember to follow through on your promises?	* Quit early when it's obvious the prize is too small?
	* Prioritise the few things that matter most, not the many things that matter less?
	* Complete high-leverage tasks first?
	* Pass on self-motivation advice to your people?

About Karlssen

Karlssen is a business-to-business telemarketing agency that acts on behalf of its clients to fill salespeople's diaries with high quality, well qualified sales appointments. Karlssen offers a low risk, high return way of quickly building a great sales pipeline and growing revenue.

For further information visit the Karlssen website.

www.karlssen.com

Karlssen One Page Guides

A range of free materials, including a series of handy one page guides for salespeople, are available from the Karlssen website.

- The series includes:
- Technique checklist
- Telemarketing stages
- Writing a cold calling script
- Questions checklist
- Handling gatekeepers
- Your telephone voice
- Qualifying prospects

www.karlssen.com

Index

20, 70, 10 rule, 47
Achievable, 16
Achievements, 51, 56
Al Fayed, Mohammed, 67
Allocating work, 29
Anger, 53, 55
Appraisals. *See* Performance
   appraisals
Aubrey, Gavin, 73
Authenticity, 38
Barrier to competition, 69
Behaviour, 14, 23, 44, 51, 54, 55,
   56
Big potatoes, 70, 71
Blind Date, 32
Bob Etherington, 70
Bonus, 17, 18, 41, 56
Boots, 66
Bored, 61
Burning platform, 44
Caan, James, 32
Calendar. *See* Diary
Career advancement, 41
Carrot and stick, 43
Coercion, 14
Cold Calling for Chickens, 70
Commission, 17, 22, 33, 56, 60
Complacency, 22, 44
Conditions, 14, 59, 76
Corporation, 21, 32
Crime and punishment, 25

Criticism, 54, 55, 56
Culture, 43, 44
Deadlines, 51, 63, 64, 70
Delegation, 58, 59, 64
Demotivators, 22
Desirable, 16
Diary, 33, 34, 55, 59, 63
Dragons Den, 32
Dunkirk, 44
Edison, Thomas, 65
Energy, 13, 18, 21, 33, 48, 51,
   58, 59, 60, 62, 68, 70, 72
Etherington, Bob, 70
Excrement, 73
Expectation management, 58
Extra-curricular, 34
Failure, 64, 65
Farmers, 30
Fear, 15, 43, 44, 55
Feedback, 54, 56, 68
Fun, 14, 31, 32, 53, 62, 64, 68
Gavin Aubrey, 73
General Electric, 47, 65
Getting a life, 61
Getting organised, 61
Gladwell, Malcolm, 65
Google, 33
Greed, 15
Harrods, 66, 67
Hierarchy, 41
High leverage, 71, 72

High-flyers, 48
Hours in the day, 47
Hunters, 30
Incentive. *See* Incentives
Incentives, 9, 14, 15, 16, 18, 29,
   31, 38, 42, 43, 45, 47, 49, 57,
   58, 59, 76
Inertia, 53, 60
Jack Welch, 43, 47
James Caan, 32
Job satisfaction, 15, 29, 42, 44,
   49, 54, 76
Joy, 20, 39
Karlssen, 4, 16, 23, 30, 83, 85
King, Will, 66
Laggards, 47, 48
Leadership, 43, 48, 51, 58, 59, 76
Levers, 15, 49, 76
Line management, 42
Losers, 64, 76
Malcolm Gladwell, 65
Management, 42
Mars, 31
Material reward, 14, 15, 17, 18,
   19, 20, 23, 31, 35, 48, 49, 56,
   68, 71, 76
Memories, 75
Middle 70%, 47, 48, 61
Mohammed Al Fayed, 67
Mojo, 61
Motivated, 13, 14, 15, 16, 21,
   29, 30, 48, 54, 59, 61, 63, 64,
   76, *See* Motivation

Motivation, 15, 17, 18, 19, 20,
   40, 43, 51, 53, 76
Neil Fiore, 44, 64
New business development, 30
non-standard rewards, 35
Obstacles, 13, 61
One page guides, 85
Outliers, 65
Overwhelmed, 61, 70
Ownership, 39
Packed lunches, 32
Pampering, 22, 26
Pecking order, 37
Performance appraisals, 56
Plan, 31, 52, 58
Positive thinking, 73
Practising, 65
Praise, 38, 39, 41, 54
Priorities, 51, 59, 64, 71
Prison, 31
Prize, 16, 19, 33, 69
Prizes, 15, 17
Procrastination, 62
Project plan, 63
Promises, 58
promotion, 41, 42
Promotion, 41, 42
Proportionate, 16
Quitting, 69
Recognition, 38, 39
Red letter days, 35
Relevant, 16
Rituals, 57, 60
River of excrement, 73

Role model, 51
Salary, 22
Sales meetings, 59, 62
Security, 15, 43, 49, 54, 76
Self esteem, 37
Self motivation, 61, 64, 76
Seriousness, 42, 53, 61
Seth Godin, 33, 68, 69
Short-term, 18, 56
Simple, 18, 19
Sports, 13, 65
Status, 15, 16, 37, 49, 54, 62, 76
Stool pigeon, 57
Strategy, 13, 58
Subconscious, 74, 75
Targets, 18, 20, 21, 22, 23, 53, 61, 66
Team spirit, 33
Telemarketing, 83
Tennis, 16

The Dip, 66, 67, 68, 69
Think Training, 73
Thomas Edison, 65
Time management, 58, 59, 61, 63, 64, 70, 71
Traditions, 32
Unachievable, 21, 22, 69
Uncapped reward, 27
Urgency, 14, 44
Values, 43
Visualising, 75
Waterstone's, 40
Welch, Jack, 43, 47, 48
White board, 34
Will King, 66
Wimbledon, 16
Winners, 64
Winning, 13, 16, 30, 31, 56, 61, 76

www.ingramcontent.com/pod-product-compliance
Lightning Source LLC
Chambersburg PA
CBHW071245170526
45165CB00003B/1244